Upper Columbia Basin Network
Limber Pine Community Dynamics 2011
Annual Monitoring Report

UPPER COLUMBIA
BASIN NETWORK
UCBN

Craters of the Moon National Monument and Preserve

Natural Resource Data Series NPS/UCBN/NRDS—2012/266

Devin S. Stucki

National Park Service
Upper Columbia Basin Network Inventory and Monitoring Program
Craters of the Moon National Monument and Preserve
Arco, ID 83213

Thomas J. Rodhouse

National Park Service
Upper Columbia Basin Network Inventory and Monitoring Program
63095 Deschutes Market Road
Bend, Oregon 97701

March 2012

U.S. Department of the Interior
National Park Service
Natural Resource Stewardship and Science
Fort Collins, Colorado

The National Park Service, Natural Resource Stewardship and Science office in Fort Collins, Colorado publishes a range of reports that address natural resource topics of interest and applicability to a broad audience in the National Park Service and others in natural resource management, including scientists, conservation and environmental constituencies, and the public.

The Natural Resource Data Series is intended for the timely release of basic data sets and data summaries. Care has been taken to assure accuracy of raw data values, but a thorough analysis and interpretation of the data has not been completed. Consequently, the initial analyses of data in this report are provisional and subject to change.

All manuscripts in the series receive the appropriate level of peer review to ensure that the information is scientifically credible, technically accurate, appropriately written for the intended audience, and designed and published in a professional manner. Data in this report were collected and analyzed using methods based on established, peer-reviewed protocols and were analyzed and interpreted within the guidelines of the protocols.

Views, statements, findings, conclusions, recommendations, and data in this report do not necessarily reflect views and policies of the National Park Service, U.S. Department of the Interior. Mention of trade names or commercial products does not constitute endorsement or recommendation for use by the U.S. Government.

This report is available from the Upper Columbia Basin Network Inventory and Monitoring Program at (http://science.nature.nps.gov/im/units/ucbn/) and the Natural Resource Publications Management website (http://www.nature.nps.gov/publications/nrpm/) on the internet.

Please cite this publication as:

Stucki, D. S., and T. J. Rodhouse. 2012. Upper Columbia Basin Network limber pine community dynamics 2011 annual monitoring report: Craters of the Moon National Monument and Preserve. Natural Resource Data Series NPS/UCBN/NRDS—2012/266. National Park Service, Fort Collins, Colorado.

NPS 131/113235, March 2012

Contents

Figures

Tables

Executive Summary

Limber pine (*Pinus flexilis*) at Craters of the Moon National Monument and Preserve (CRMO) is one of 14 vital signs identified in the long-term monitoring plan for the Upper Columbia Basin Network (UCBN). Vital signs are indicators of ecosystem health which represent a broad suite of ecological phenomena operating across multiple temporal and spatial scales. Vital signs were selected to meet the needs of park management and also to detect responses to unanticipated environmental conditions and management issues in the future. Limber pine is one of several white pine species susceptible to the invasive pathogen white pine blister rust (*Cronartium ribicola*) which has decimated stands throughout the Intermountain West and portions of the Pacific West. Limber pine trees are vulnerable to invasive pathogens as well as other stressors including native pathogens and climate-change induced drought and have been recognized as a high priority vital sign for CRMO. Although pathogen and insect infestations at CRMO are currently not high, declining trends in some populations observed in white pine populations in the Cascade and Rocky Mountain ranges, coupled with the identification of incipient blister rust and mountain pine beetle infestations in the park, is cause for significant concern about the future status of these valuable communities. Monitoring limber pine community dynamics will allow CRMO to detect changes in the ecological condition of this community and perhaps to initiate more effective management intervention. Monitoring information from this project will also contribute meaningfully to the broader regional assessment of the status and trend of white pine species across western North America. Limber pine monitoring in CRMO is being closely coordinated with high-elevation whitebark pine (*Pinus albicaulis*) and foxtail pine (*Pinus balfouriana*) monitoring in the Klamath and Sierra Nevada Networks, which includes the use of a common protocol (McKinney et al. *in revision*).

Protocol implementation began at CRMO with the installation of the first of three rotating panels, each consisting of a random sample of 30 permanent 50 x 50 m (2500 m^2) plots, in June-July, 2011. Two additional plots were also established and surveyed, for a total of 32 plots, and these will be incorporated into panel 2 during the 2013 field season. The data collected from this monitoring program will be used to quantify limber pine forest dynamics as identified in the monitoring objectives, i.e., species composition and structure, birth, death and growth rates, cone production, and the incidence of infection and infection severity by white pine blister rust, pine beetles, and dwarf mistletoe.

In 2011, no incidences of white pine blister rust or mountain pine beetle attacks were found within the sampled plots, although there is an active blister rust infection in a small stand of limber pine trees in the north end of the monument. Dwarf mistletoe was found in 26% of the live limber pine trees. There were no active signs of mountain pine beetle infestation, although park staff report an increasing frequency of beetle-killed limber pine trees scattered throughout the northern portion of the monument. The average number of limber pine trees per plot was only 13 with a maximum of 73 trees. Seventy-one percent of live limber pine trees (*n*=413) had produced female cones. These results provide important baseline descriptions of CRMO's unique limber pine population, which occurs on the lower elevation periphery of the species' range.

Acknowledgments

Funding for this project was provided through the National Park Service Natural Resource Challenge and the Servicewide Inventory and Monitoring Program. We thank the park superintendents and resource staff who met with us to discuss park management objectives and information needs, and who provided invaluable logistical support to field operations in 2011. Shawn McKinney provided helpful comments during the preparation of this report. We also thank Dan Esposito, Matt Nolte, and Jim Syvertsen for their efforts in gathering the data presented in this publication.

Background and Objectives

Many western North American coniferous forests are currently facing unprecedented health challenges, including upsurges of native pests and pathogens, invasive exotic species, and altered disturbance regimes. Increased atmospheric warming, carbon dioxide concentration, and nitrogen deposition, as well as changes in precipitation patterns (i.e., timing, magnitude, and type) pose additional short- and long-term threats. Each factor alone can alter forest ecosystem structure, function, and species composition, while additive or synergistic effects are possible if multiple agents act jointly. How forest ecosystems will respond to modern perturbations is uncertain, however the magnitude of change in structure and composition, and key ecological processes will likely be exceptional. Indeed, increased tree mortality rates over the last several decades have recently been documented across a broad range of latitude and forest types in western North America (van Mantgem et al. 2009).

Five-needle white pines (Family Pinaceae, Genus *Pinus*, Subgenus *Strobus*), and in particular whitebark pine, limber pine, and foxtail pine, are foundational species (Tomback and Achuff 2010) in upper subalpine and treeline forests of several National Park Service (NPS) Pacific West Region (PWR) parks, including Craters of the Moon National Monument and Preserve (CRMO). Ongoing declines of many foundation tree species pose an especially compelling problem because these species provide fundamental structure to a system and are thereby irreplaceable (Ellison et al. 2005). Foundation species generally occupy low trophic levels, create locally stable conditions required by many other species, and stabilize fundamental ecosystem processes (Ellison et al. 2005). In temperate zone forests (e.g., western North America) there often are only one or two foundational tree species, and therefore little functional redundancy is present in the system. If a foundation tree species is lost from these systems, it will likely lead to a cascade of secondary losses, shifts in biological diversity, and ultimately affect the functioning and stability of the community (Ebenman and Jonsson 2005).

Limber pine (*Pinus flexilis* James) occurs in areas throughout the Rocky Mountains, including parks within the UCBN, and extends to the east side of the Sierra Nevada (Figure 1). The species occupies a wide elevation range, and therefore occurs in lower treeline as well as upper subalpine and treeline habitats. By virtue of its status as a dominant component of forest stands, limber pine can have a large influence on key ecosystem processes and community dynamics, such as influencing snowmelt and stream flow, moderating local environments allowing for establishment of shade-tolerant plants, and providing habitat and food resources for birds and mammals. Limber pine is a pioneer of severe sites, moderating local environments and facilitating the establishment of other species (Baumeister and Callaway 2006). Limber pine cones open when seeds are ripe; some seeds remain within cones, while others fall to the ground. The seeds of limber pine are large, have rudimentary wings, and are prized by numerous birds and mammals. Its seeds are dispersed by Clark's nutcrackers and small mammals (Vander Wall 1988, Tomback et al. 2005).

Limber pine forms monotypic woodlands in much of the northern, highest-elevation portions of CRMO, and also occurs with Rocky Mountain juniper (*Juniperus scopulorum*) in some areas of the park. Limber pine contributes significantly to the biodiversity of CRMO, and is an integral part of the park's striking landscape. The presence of limber pine woodlands in CRMO dramatically contributes to visitor experience in addition to its important ecological significance. Despite the broad physiological tolerance exhibited by limber pine to harsh environmental conditions, the CRMO limber pine population is clearly unique in that it is growing at the very limits of its physiological tolerance and therefore provides an important opportunity for ecological learning.

There is no history of formal inventory and monitoring of the CRMO limber pine population. During the 1960's, park policy included removal and girdling of pines infected with dwarf mistletoe in the vicinity of the park visitor center and along the park loop road which penetrates the northern portion of the lava flows. Beginning in 2006, CRMO initiated informal surveys of limber pine stands for early detection of white pine blister rust infection. There has been a hope that the aridity of the park will slow or prevent blister rust infection, but in 2006, three infected trees with active cankers were found and removed. Subsequent surveys have confirmed a small but well-established infection in several trees in the same stand. During 2011 pre-season field training, we photographed active cankers in several limber pine trees in this stand.

In 2009, we initiated a small pilot survey of six limber pine stands in CRMO following the *Interagency Whitebark Pine Monitoring Protocol for the Greater Yellowstone Ecosystem* (Greater Yellowstone Whitebark Pine Monitoring Working Group [hereafter referred to as GYWPMWG] 2007). No blister rust was found during that survey, although mountain pine beetle galleries were found in several trees, and dwarf mistletoe was ubiquitous. In 2010 we tested a draft version of the protocol currently being used by the Upper Columbia Basin Network (UCBN), as well as the Klamath Network (KLMN) and Sierra Nevada Network (SIEN; McKinney et al. *in revision*). The results reported in this report were generated in 2011 with data collected following an updated protocol by McKinney et al. (*in revision*). This is the first formal year of protocol implementation, and the permanent plots established in 2011 represent the first of 3 "panels" of plots that will be monitored into the future.

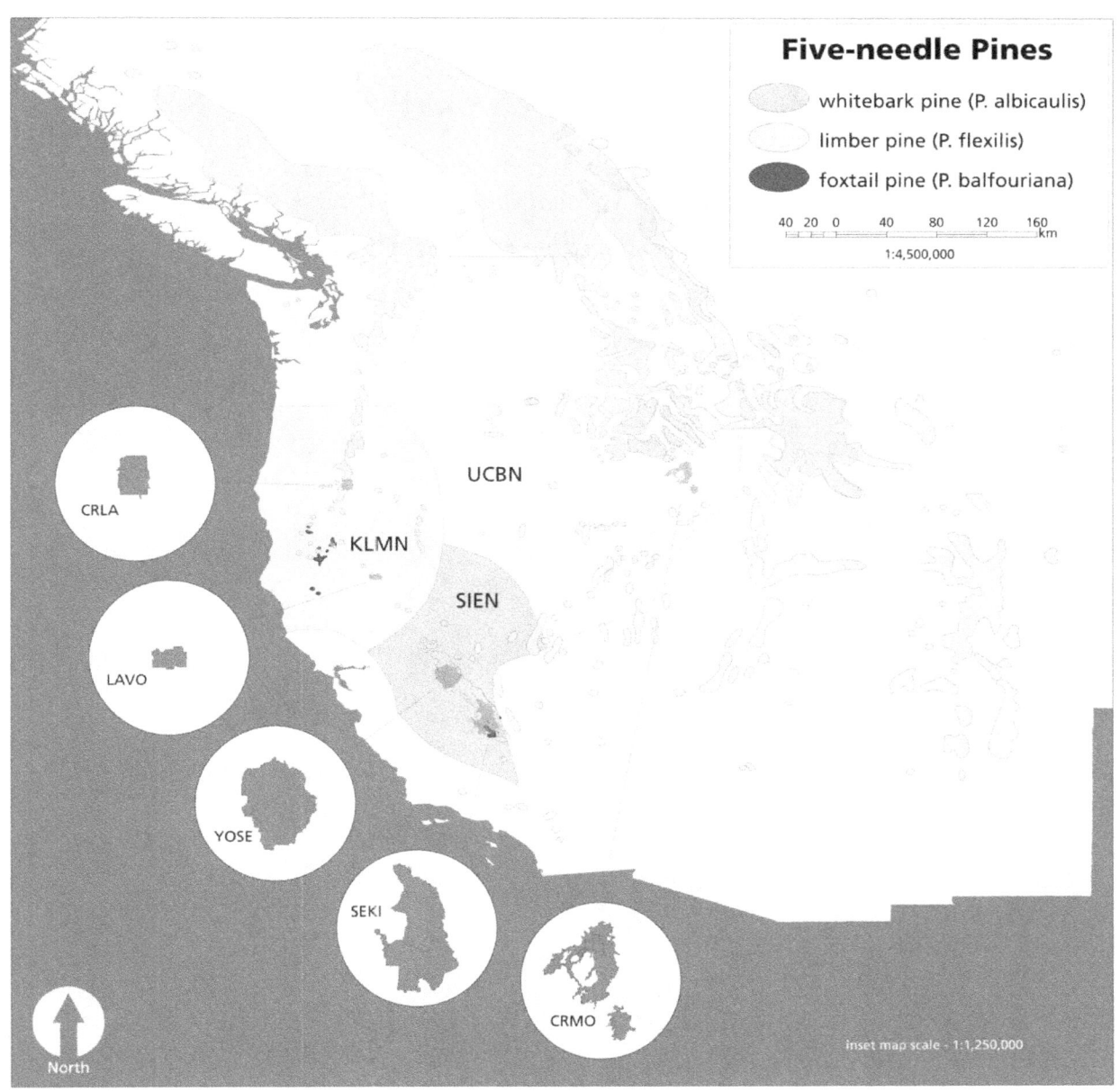

Figure 1. Distribution of whitebark pine, limber pine, and foxtail pine (from Little 1971) and locations of three Pacific West Region networks and associated parks.

Objectives

Limber pine monitoring objectives were established through a collaborative process with ecologists from KLMN, SIEN, and the UCBN as part of a collaborative white pine monitoring protocol (McKinney et al. *in revision*). The objectives were also linked to the vital signs that were developed by each network and documented in network monitoring plans (Garrett et al. 2007, Sarr et al. 2007, Mutch et al. 2008). The anticipated impacts of blister rust, dwarf mistletoe, mountain pine beetle, and climate change to high-elevation pines based on published scientific literature and expert opinion were driving factors as well. Through an approach which involves monitoring individual trees within permanent plots, there will be an ability to estimate key demographic parameters within white pine forest types. Our objectives are to detect status and trend in:

1. Trees species composition and structure

2. Tree species birth, death, and grow rates

3. Incidence of white pine blister rust (*Cronartium ribicola*) and level of crown kill

4. Incidence of pine beetle (*Dendroctonus spp.*) and severity of tree damage

5. Incidence of dwarf mistletoe (*Arceuthobium spp.*) and severity of tree damage

6. Cone production of white pine species

Methods

This section provides a detailed summary of the methods used for limber pine monitoring in CRMO. For the complete methodology of limber pine monitoring refer to the collaborative white pine monitoring protocol for networks in the Pacific West Region (McKinney et al. *in revision*).

Sampling Frame

Limber pine monitoring plots have been established within portions of two of three limber pine plant associations mapped at CRMO (Bell et al. 2009): *P. flexilis/Purshia tridentata* Woodland, and *P. flexilis/Artemisia spp.* Woodland. A third sparsely vegetated and largely inaccessible association found across the interior of the lava flow, *P. flexilis/Chamaebatiaria millefolium/Poa secunda* Sparse Vegetation (Belle et al. 2009), was excluded from the sampling frame (McKinney et al. *in revision*). The *P. flexilis/Purshia tridentata* Woodland association is endemic to the Snake River Plain in Idaho and has been identified as critically imperiled by NatureServe (G1 ranking; Bell et al. 2009). The sampling frame includes all of these two *P. flexilis* woodland associations that occur within 2 km of a road and trail, excluding excessively steep areas with > 35 degrees slope and also excluding the southern portion of the Wilderness Trail which extends beyond the 2 km buffer from the southern portion of CRMO's loop road (Figure 2). The 2 km buffer was chosen to reduce crew exposure to unsafe travel across lava flows and potential accident response time, to reduce overall crew travel costs, and to ensure that sample sizes could be achieved each season. Although constrained, this sampling frame still encompasses 1,260 ha (20%) of the woodland associations in CRMO, capturing a substantial and representative proportion of *P. flexilis* woodlands within the park. The landscape at CRMO is relatively flat but there is a significant elevation gradient from south to north. The sampling frame contains a substantial portion of this gradient with elevations ranging from 1605-1900 m and Figure 3 shows a histogram of the elevations captured by the sample of plot locations. Elevation is a proxy for the effects of temperature and precipitation (Körner 2007), and sampling along the elevational gradient will enable hypotheses about the effects of climate on limber pine demography and rust infection dynamics to be addressed. Furthermore, the elevation gradient represented by the sample closely matches the one also captured by the UCBN's pika monitoring protocol in CRMO (Jeffress et al. 2011), facilitating integrated assessment of climate change impacts on these two climate-sensitive sentinel populations in the future.

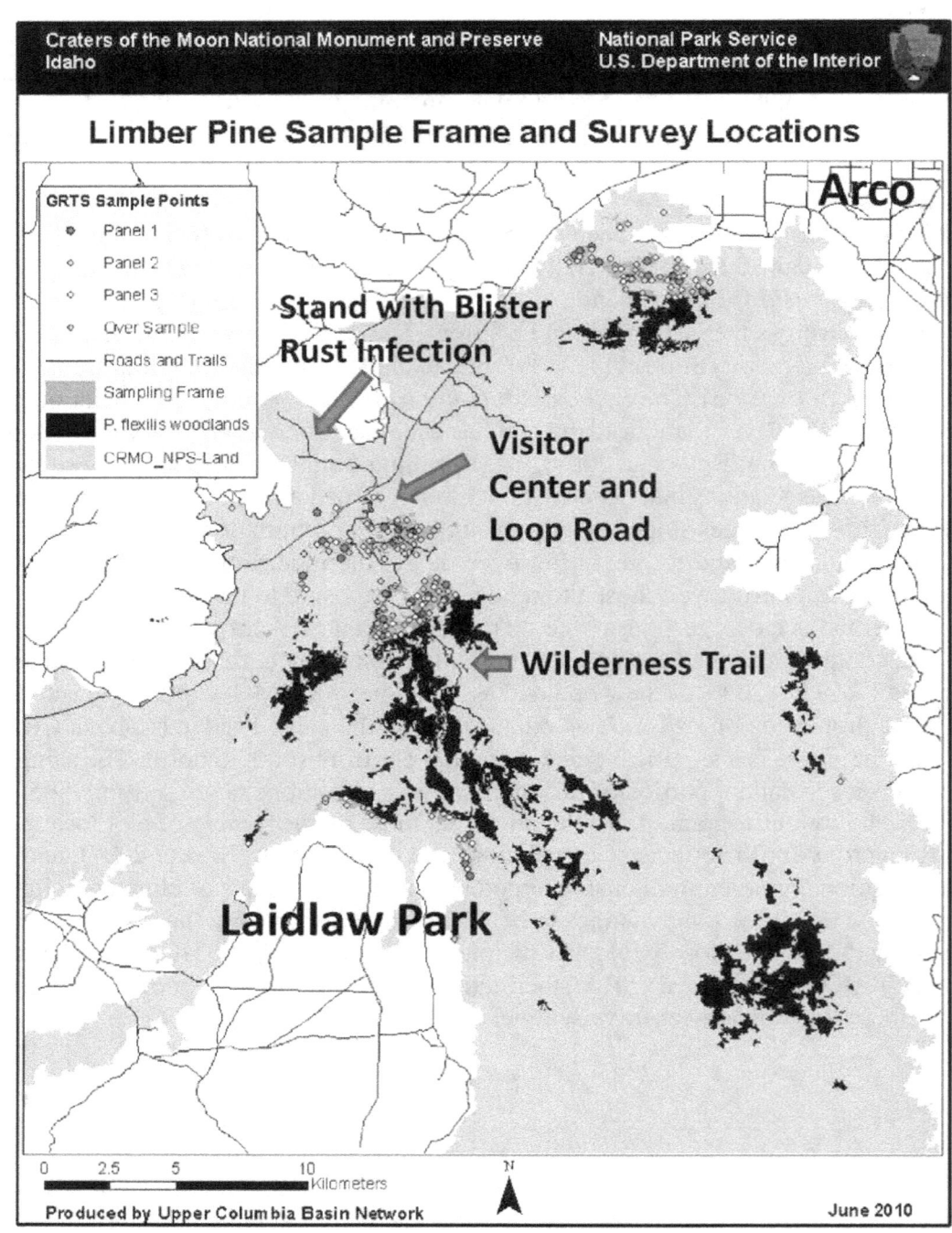

Figure 2. Limber pine monitoring sampling frame and GRTS sample of plot point locations within Craters of the Moon National Monument and Preserve. The sample frame (green) includes all areas of the park within 2 km of roads and trails that have been mapped by Bell et al. (2009) as *P. flexilis* woodland. Sample locations are separated into three equal panels of 30 points each of which will be visited once every three years in a rotating panel sampling design. The first year's panel of 30 points is illustrated in red. An oversample of points was also drawn using the GRTS algorithm to support any eventual site additions, deletions, or replacements.

Figure 3. Histogram of elevations represented in the GRTS sample (*n*=90) for Craters of the Moon National Monument and Preserve.

The sites to be sampled have been identified using a randomized spatially-balanced sampling design via the Generalized Random Tessellation Stratified (GRTS) algorithm (Stevens and Olsen 2004). This design assigns permanent plots to random locations within the sampling frame while keeping the order of plots sampled unstructured and of equal-probability, as well as spatially balanced. This method allows for the addition of new sites or replacement sites which is useful in eliminating sampling difficulties that arise from site inaccessibility or sampling frame errors where, for instance, an unsuitable habitat type was erroneously mapped as suitable.

Frequency and Timing of Sampling

We have adopted a three-year rotating panel design for re-surveying permanent plots in CRMO. The sample of 90 plots in CRMO has been subdivided into three panels, each revisited once per three-year rotation cycle (a $[1-2^3]$ design, *sensu* MacDonald 2003; Table 1). Appendix 1 lists all 30 panel 1 plots plus oversamples that were evaluated and established for monitoring in 2011. Two extra oversample plots (numbers 96 and 99, Appendix 1) were also established and surveyed in 2011 and these will be resurveyed and incorporated into panel 2 in 2013. In 2011 all plots were sampled between June 26 and July 26.

Table 1. Revisit design for monitoring limber pine in the Upper Columbia Basin Network. Each panel consists of 30 plots. Panels are visited once per 3-year rotation, yielding a total sample size of 90 plots.

Panel	Year												
	2011	2012	2013	2014	2015	2016	2017	2018	2019	2020	2021	2022	2023
1 (n = 30)	x			x			x			x			x
2 (n = 30)		x			x			x			x		
3 (n = 30)			x			x			x			x	

Plot Layout

Macroplots, consisting of five (5) subplots, and containing nine (9) seedling/sapling regeneration plots are used to measure and track forest demographic parameters, disease and insect occurrence, and magnitude of their impact. The response design for this protocol is compatible with the *Interagency Whitebark Pine Monitoring Protocol for the Greater Yellowstone Ecosystem* (GYWPMWG 2007) but differs in some respects, most notably, plot size. The 10 x 50 m plot size from the Yellowstone protocol has been increased to accommodate the often sparse distribution of white pines in our PWR parks and to adequately address forest demographic objectives. The UCBN uses a 50 x 50 m plot (0.25 ha or 2,500 m^2) following analyses of pilot data collected in network parks in 2009–2010 (Figure 4; McKinney et al. *in revision*). This design effectively represents five parallel 10 x 50 m plots as used in the GRYN and as proposed by the Whitebark Pine Ecosystem Foundation (Tomback et al. 2005).

A total of nine square regeneration plots (3 x 3 m) are established for each 50 x 50 m macroplot to measure seedling regeneration (Figure 4). Regeneration subplots are located near each corner (4), at each midpoint between corners (4), and in the middle (1) of the macroplot (Figure 4). The current design was chosen because it provides a reasonable balance among sampling time constraints, observer accuracy and precision and total area sampled.

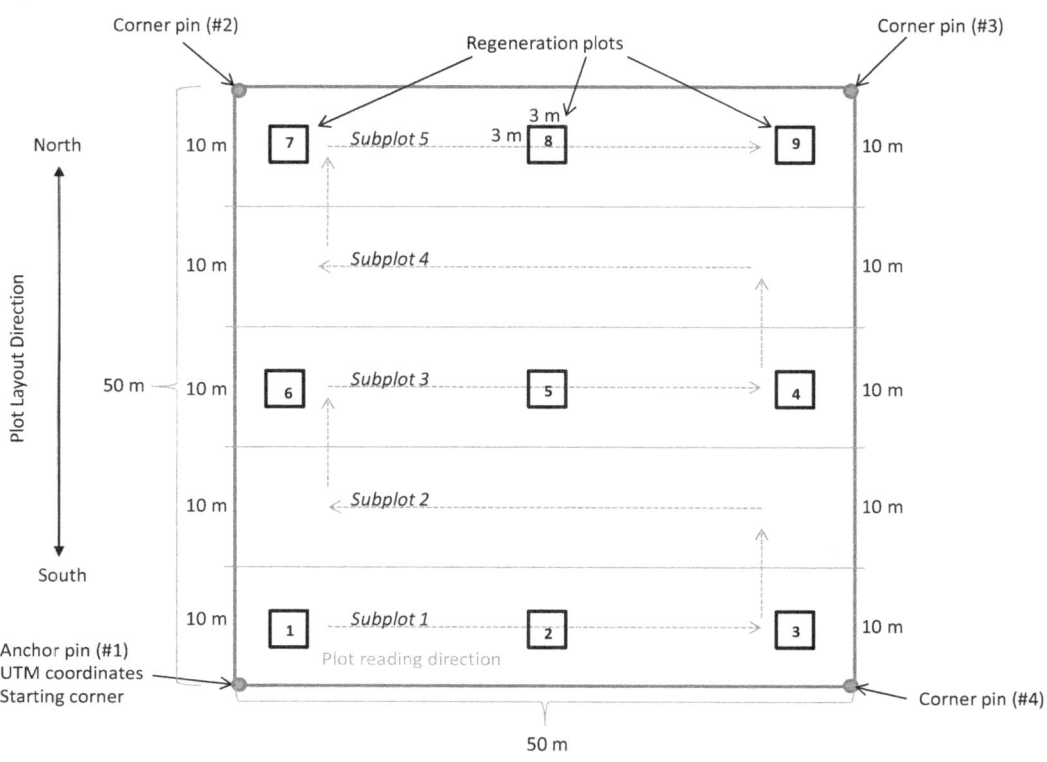

Figure 4. 50 x 50 m macroplot plot with five 10 x 50 m subplots, and nine 3 x 3 m regeneration plots used in SIEN and UCBN white pine monitoring.

Plot Measurements

Table 2 outlines the relationship among the variables, raw data, summarized data, and monitoring objectives. Detailed instructions on response design measurements are provided by McKinney et al. (*in revision*) and only a general overview is presented here.

Each live tree taller than 1.37 m has a uniquely numbered metal tag attached to it, its species identified, and diameter at 1.37 m (breast height, dbh) and height measured. Dead trees are tagged and are distinguished between recently dead and dead. Recently dead trees have red needles present (but no green needles) and dead trees have no needles present. White pine blister rust infection is assessed for all living white pine trees. The bole and branches of white pine trees are each vertically divided into thirds (upper, middle, and bottom) and each third is assigned one of three rust condition classes: 1) absent–no sign of rust infection, 2) active cankers (aeciospores present), or 3) no active cankers, but with the presence of three of the following five indicators of infection: rodent chewing, flagging, swelling, roughened bark, and oozing sap. Mountain pine beetle occurrence is recorded for all pine trees using three indicators of beetle activity: pitch tubes, frass, and J-shaped galleries. The presence of galleries is only determined for recently dead and dead trees because bark has to be removed for this assessment. Dwarf mistletoe infection is recorded for all living white pine trees by noting presence or absence for each third of a tree. The level of canopy kill in live white pine trees is determined by dividing the tree's canopy (all the main branches that begin as bifurcations off the bole, encompassing all foliage and supporting twigs and side branches) into thirds and ocularly estimating the percentage of each third that is dead. Cone production is recorded as to whether female cones are present or absent on each white pine tree. Live seedlings are tallied by species and height class in regeneration plots. Height classes are 1) 20 to <50 cm; 2) 50 to <100 cm; and 3) 100 to <137 cm.

Table 2. Relationship among variables, data, and objectives, from McKinney et al. (*in revision*).

Variable	Raw Data	Summarized Data	Objectives Addressed
Species	Tree (nominal)	Trees per hectare (TPH); all spp., each spp., proportion of total by spp.	1. composition & structure
Diameter	Tree (cm)	Basal area (m²/ha); all spp., each spp., proportion of total by spp. Mean diameter (cm) by spp. Diameter classes (5 cm); proportion and TPH by spp.	1. composition & structure 2. growth rate
Height	Tree (m)	Mean ht. (m); all spp. and by each spp. Height classes (3 m); proportion and TPH by spp.	1. composition & structure 2. growth rate
Status	Tree (live or dead)	Proportion live and dead; all spp and by each sp. TPH and proportion by 5 cm diameter classes in each condition; all spp and by each sp.	2. birth and death rates
Crown kill	Each of three parts of a tree (%)	Mean (%); individual trees, each sp, and all spp.	3. level of crown kill
Active canker	Each of three parts of a tree (p/a)	Proportion and TPH with active cankers by each white pine sp.	3. rust infection incidence
Inactive canker	Each of three parts of a tree (p/a)	Proportion and TPH with inactive cankers by each white pine sp.	3. rust infection incidence
Rust infection	Tree (p/a of active or inactive canker)	Proportion and TPH infected and healthy by each white pine sp. TPH by 5 cm diameter classes in each condition by each white pine sp.	3. rust infection incidence
Bark beetle	Tree (p/a)	Proportion and TPH with beetle sign; all spp and each sp.	4. incidence of bark beetle
Dwarf mistletoe	Tree (p/a)	Proportion and TPH with mistletoe sign; all spp and each sp.	5. incidence of dwarf mistletoe
Female cones	Tree (p/a)	Proportion and TPH with cones by each white pine sp.	6. cone production
Seedlings	9 m² plot; number of each of three size classes by species	Mean (number per m²); all spp and each sp for each size class.	1. composition & structure 2. birth rates

Results and Discussion

In 2011 we installed and sampled 32 plots in Craters of the Moon (Appendix 1), including two additional oversample plots that will be incorporated into panel 2 but that are included in the results reported here. These 32 plots contained a total of 415 limber pine trees, 39 Rocky Mountain juniper trees, 58 Douglas-fir (*Pseudotsuga menziesii*) trees. They also contained 32 dead trees, 2 of which were identified as limber pine and 30 that were not identified to species. No limber pine trees were found with signs of blister rust infection in plots. However, there is active blister rust infection in a small stand of limber pine trees at the north end of the monument, discovered in 2006 (Figure 2). We visited this stand during training in 2011 and photographed active sporulating cankers. No live limber pine trees showed signs of attack by pine beetles, but 26% of live limber pine trees in CRMO were infected with dwarf mistletoe. In general, limber pine stands in this arid lava landscape are rather sparsely populated. The average number of limber pine trees per 2500 m^2 plot was only 13, and never exceeded 73 trees; 71% of live *P. flexilis* trees (n=413) produced female cones. Additional summary statistics are reported in Table 3. Figure 5 shows live *P. flexilis* basal area per plot (m^2/plot) and the number of live *P. flexilis* infected with mistletoe along the elevational gradient captured by the 2011 survey. There does not appear to be a relationship between elevation and basal area at this time, but a relationship between elevation and mistletoe infection may be present. This and other similar kinds of simple graphical analyses will become more informative after additional panels of plots have been surveyed.

Field experience, including the week-long training held jointly by the UCBN and SIEN at CRMO, as well as these preliminary results indicate that the monitoring effort is off to a good start with a protocol well suited for this park. Conversations with US Forest Service forest pathologists familiar with the CRMO limber pine population as well as limber pine populations in the Pioneer Mountains north of CRMO have underscored the importance of this monitoring effort to the broader scientific community-at-large (Jim Hoffman and Carl Jorgensen, US Forest Service, personal communication). The CRMO population occurs at the lower elevation periphery of the species' physiological tolerance in Idaho, and therefore studying the dynamics of this population over time can inform questions about how the species may respond to drought and other climatic events that are expected to become more frequent and intense under projected climate change. This information will also be integral for management strategies concerned with these issues in the future. The preliminary results from 2011 underscore several unique characteristics of the population. The sparse distribution of limber pine in stands is striking, as is the high levels of mistletoe infection. The endemic but low-level infestation of mountain pine beetle in the population is also noteworthy. These characteristics are apparently quite different from limber pine populations growing at higher elevations in the mountains of central Idaho (Jim Hoffman, US Forest Service, personal communication). Long-term monitoring will be important to provide a more comprehensive understanding of the population and to provide early detection of significant changes and trends that may require management intervention.

Table 3. Summary table of 2011 results for CRMO limber pine monitoring. Standard deviations are provided in parentheses where appropriate.

Metric	Status[1]
Number of established plots	32.00 (na)
Average live *Pinus flexilis* basal area (m^2/ha)	1.39 (1.50)
Average live *Pseudotsuga menziesii* basal area (m^2/ha)	0.70 (0.00)
Average live *Juniperus scopulorum* basal area (m^2/ha)	0.13 (0.87)
Average number of *J. scopulorum* trees/ha	19.50 (20.22)
Average number of *P. flexilis* trees/ha	51.63 (63.03)
Average number of *P. menziesii* trees/ha	232.00 (na)
Blister Rust Infection Rate (%)	0.00 (0.00)
Dwarf Mistletoe Infection Rate (%)	26.15 (0.60)
Mountain Pine Beetle Infection Rate (%)	0.00 (0.00)
Avg. regeneration of *J. scopulorum* 20-50cm (seedlings/m^2/macroplot, *n*=8)	0.000 (0.000)
Avg. regeneration of *J. scopulorum* 50-100cm (seedlings/m^2/macroplot, *n*=8)	0.000 (0.000)
Avg. regeneration of *J. scopulorum*) 100-137cm (seedlings/m^2/macroplot, *n*=8)	0.001 (0.004)
Avg. regeneration of *P. flexilis* 20-50cm (seedlings/m^2/macroplot, *n*=32)	0.004 (0.009)
Avg. regeneration of *P. flexilis* 50-100cm (seedlings/m^2/macroplot, *n*=32)	0.004 (0.014)
Avg. regeneration of *P. flexilis* 100-137cm (seedlings/m^2/macroplot, *n*=32)	0.000 (0.000)
Avg. regeneration of *P. menziesii* 20-50cm (seedlings/m^2/macroplot, *n*=1)	0.062 (na)
Avg. regeneration of *P. menziesii* 50-100cm (seedlings/m^2/macroplot, *n*=1)	0.086 (na)
Avg. regeneration of *P. menziesii* 100-137cm (seedlings/m^2/macroplot, *n*=1)	0.000 (na)
Limber pine trees with female cones (%)	71.67 (0.01)

[1] Only 1 plot in 2011 with *P. menziesii* and 8 plots in 2011 with *J. scopulorum*.

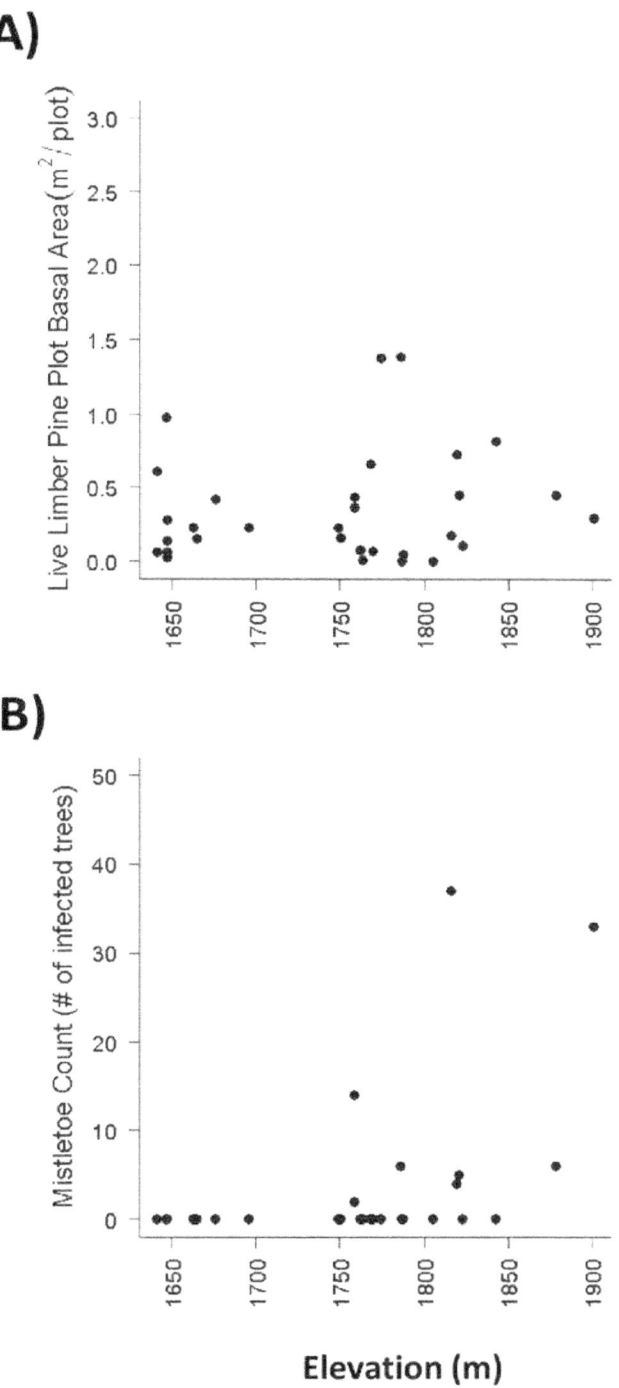

Figure 5. A) Live limber pine basal area (m^2) per plot and B) count of trees infected with mistletoe along the elevational gradient captured in the 2011 survey.

Literature Cited

Baumeister, D., and R. M. Callaway. 2006. Facilitation by *Pinus flexilis* during succession: A hierarchy of mechanisms benefits other plant species. Ecology 87:1816–1830.

Bell, J., D. Cogan, J. J. Erixson, and J. Von Loh. 2009. Vegetation inventory project report: Craters of the Moon National Monument and Preserve. Natural Resource Technical Report NPS/UCBN/NRTR—2009/277. National Park Service, Fort Collins, Colorado.

Ebenman, B., and T. Jonsson. 2005. Using community viability analysis to identify fragile systems and keystone species. Trends in Ecology and Evolution 20:568–575.

Ellison, A. E., M. S. Bank, B. D. Clinton, E. A. Colburn, K. Elliott, C. R. Ford, D. R. Foster, B. D. Kloeppel, J. D. Knoepp, G. M. Lovett, J. Mohan, D. A. Orwig, N. L. Rodenhouse, W. V. Sobczak, K. A. Stinson, J. K. Stone, C. M. Swan, J. Thompson, B. Von Holle, and J. R. Webster. 2005. Loss of foundation species: consequences for the structure and dynamics of forested ecosystems. Frontiers in Ecology and the Environment 3:479–486.

Garrett, L. K., T. J. Rodhouse, G. H. Dicus, C. C. Caudill, and M. R. Shardlow. 2007. Upper Columbia Basin Network vital signs monitoring plan. Natural Resource Report NPS/ UCBN/NRR—2007/002. National Park Service, Fort Collins, Colorado.

Greater Yellowstone Whitebark Pine Monitoring Working Group. 2007. Interagency whitebark pine monitoring protocol for the Greater Yellowstone Ecosystem, v 1.0. Greater Yellowstone Coordinating Committee, Bozeman, Montana. Unpublished.

Jeffress, M. R., J. Apel, L. K. Garrett, G. Holm, D. Larson, N. Nordensten, and T. J. Rodhouse. 2011. Monitoring the American pika (*Ochotona princeps*) in the Pacific West Region - Crater Lake National Park, Craters of the Moon National Monument and Preserve, Lassen Volcanic National Park, and Lava Beds National Monument: Narrative Version 1.0. Natural Resource Report NPS/UCBN/NRR—2011/336. National Park Service, Fort Collins, Colorado.

Körner, C. 2007. The use of 'altitude' in ecological research. Trends in Ecology and Evolution 22:569–574.

Little, E. L., Jr. 1971. Conifers and important hardwoods. Volume 1 of Atlas of United States trees. U.S. Department of Agriculture Miscellaneous Publication 1146.

McDonald, T. L. 2003. Review of environmental monitoring methods: Survey designs. Environmental Monitoring and Assessment 85:277–292.

McKinney, S. T., T. Rodhouse, L. Chow, A. Chung-MacCoubrey, G. Dicus, L. Garrett, K. Irvine, S. Mohren, D. Odion, D. Sarr, and L. A. Starcevich. *In revision*. Monitoring white pine (*Pinus albicaulis, P. balfouriana, P. flexilis*) community dynamics in the Pacific West Region - Klamath, Sierra Nevada, and Upper Columbia Basin Networks: Narrative and

Standard Operating Procedures (bound separately) version 1.0. Natural Resource Report NPS/PWRO/ NRR—2011/XXX. National Park Service, Fort Collins, Colorado.

Mutch, L. S., M. G. Rose, A. M. Heard, R. R. Cook, and G. L. Entsminger. 2008. Sierra Nevada Network vital signs monitoring plan. Natural Resource Report NPS/ SIEN/NRR—2008/072. National Park Service, Fort Collins, Colorado.

Sarr, D. A., D. C. Odion, S. R. Mohren, E. E. Perry, R. L. Hoffman, L. K. Bridy, and A. A. Merton. 2007. Vital signs monitoring plan for the Klamath Network: Phase III report. Natural Resource Technical Report NPS/KLMN/NRR—2007/016, National Park Service, Fort Collins, Colorado.

Stevens, D. L., and A. R. Olsen. 2004. Spatially balanced sampling of natural resources. Journal of the American Statistical Association 99:262–278.

Tomback, D. F., A. W. Schoettle, K. E. Chevalier, and C. A. Jones. 2005. Life on the Edge for limber pine: Seed dispersal within peripheral population. Ecoscience 12:519-529.

Tomback, D. F., and P. Achuff. 2010. Blister rust and western forest biodiversity: ecology, values, and outlook for white pines. Forest Pathology 40:186-225.

Vander Wall, S. B. 1988. Foraging of Clark's Nutcracker on rapidly changing pine seek resources. Condor 90:621-631.

van Mantgem, P. J., N. L. Stephenson, J. C. Byrne, L. D. Daniels, J. F. Franklin, P. Z. Fulé, M. E. Harmon, A. J. Larson, J. M. Smith, A. H. Taylor, T. T. Veblen. 2009. Widespread increase of tree mortality rates in the western United States. Science 323:521–523.

Appendix 1. Plots and oversamples evaluated and established for monitoring in 2011 at Craters of the Moon National Monument and Preserve (CRMO).

Table A-1. Spatially-balanced list of sampling locations for CRMO, organized by panel. Panel 1 sites sampled in 2011 are noted in EvalStatus. Oversample locations provide the replacements for sites dropped during office and field evaluation. Oversample sites 91-95 will become permanent members of panel 1. Oversample sites 96 and 99 will be rotated in to panel 2 and 3 as drops occur during implementation of those panels. Oversample plot 96 will be the first replacement used in panel 2 during 2012 sampling, followed by plot 97 and so on, in GRTS order. Note that UTM X and UTM Y are the plot corner 1 coordinates as established in the field, and no longer match exactly the coordinates produced by the GRTS algorithm used to navigate to the plot during initial set-up.

Plot ID	UTM X	UTM Y	GRTS wgt	panel	EvalStatus	EvalNotes
Site-001	301108	4825065	140103	Panel_1	Established	
Site-002	300938	4824871	140103	Panel_1	Established	
Site-003	293580	4810610	140103	Panel_1	Established	
Site-004	293666	4814204	140103	Panel_1	Established	
Site-005	301828	4824600	140103	Panel_1	Established	
Site-006	295992	4811964	140103	Panel_1	Established	
Site-007	291987	4813011	140103	Panel_1	Established	
Site-008	294159	4814128	140103	Panel_1	Established	
Site-009	303667	4824640	140103	Panel_1	Established	
Site-010	294712	4811265	140103	Panel_1	Dropped	No trees
Site-011	291291	4813692	140103	Panel_1	Established	
Site-012	296913	4800376	140103	Panel_1	Established	
Site-013	304659	4824050	140103	Panel_1	Established	
Site-014	293708	4811587	140103	Panel_1	Established	
Site-015	292100	4813409	140103	Panel_1	Established	
Site-016	296891	4801995	140103	Panel_1	Established	
Site-017	301605	4825253	140103	Panel_1	Established	
Site-018	305824	4823410	140103	Panel_1	Dropped	No trees
Site-019	295115	4810759	140103	Panel_1	Established	
Site-020	294730	4814022	140103	Panel_1	Established	
Site-021	303039	4823964	140103	Panel_1	Established	

Plot ID	UTM X	UTM Y	GRTS wgt	panel	EvalStatus	EvalNotes
Site-022	295974	4811384	140103	Panel_1	Established	
Site-023	290552	4812330	140103	Panel_1	Established	
Site-024	293947	4813626	140103	Panel_1	Established	
Site-025	303719	4824073	140103	Panel_1	Dropped	No trees
Site-026	295340	4811495	140103	Panel_1	Dropped	No trees
Site-027	291079	4814801	140103	Panel_1	Established	
Site-028	296718	4800891	140103	Panel_1	Established	
Site-029	304915	4823823	140103	Panel_1	Dropped	No trees
Site-030	293565	4809910	140103	Panel_1	Established	
Site-091	293447	4810025	140103	OverSamp	Established	Replace site 10
Site-092	294173	4813653	140103	OverSamp	Established	Replace site 18
Site-093	304496	4823236	140103	OverSamp	Established	Replace site 25
Site-094	293645	4810962	140103	OverSamp	Established	Replace site 26
Site-095	295045	4814190	140103	OverSamp	Established	Replace site 29
Site-096	293002	4803077	140103	OverSamp	Established	Extra (Panel 2?)
Site-097	301546	4824656	140103	OverSamp	Not Evaluated	Panel 2?
Site-098	287801	4814990	140103	OverSamp	Not Evaluated	Panel 2?
Site-099	295201	4810631	140103	OverSamp	Established	Extra (Panel 2?)

Appendix 2. Suggested/required changes to the protocol

Changes to the protocol (McKinney et al. *in review*) are minimal at this time and refer to the position of the plot and the regeneration plots within it, as well as a diagram update to these changes. Plot orientation, which was originally arranged to be aligned upslope with the origin on the downhill side, has been changed so that the plot is aligned along the cardinal directions and with the plot origin now being the southwest corner and the subplots running east and west. This change was made to standardize the way that plots were oriented and to avoid confusion during plot setup in the field. Another change was made to the order of regeneration plot surveys. The numbers of the 4th and 6th regeneration plots have been reversed to facilitate more efficient sampling. Lastly, the plot layout figure (Figure 4) has been updated to address these changes.